DRAWING URBAN HEROES

**William Potter
and Juan Calle**

PowerKiDS
press

CONTENTS

URBAN HEROES UNITE

It's time to bring your wildest adventures to life! You can create heroes and villains, amazing locations, and super–cool technology to tell your comic book story.

LET'S MAKE COMICS

This book is packed with ideas and guides to help you make up your own characters for incredible adventures. We'll show you the basics for bringing your characters to life and how to put them into a comic strip for all to see.

STEPS AHEAD

We're going to focus on those city-dwelling night fighters—urban heroes. Step-by-step instructions, guides on anatomy, and **MODEL SHEETS** will show you how to draw convincing characters. You'll create exciting fight sequences, and draw realistic urban environments!

After dark, two brave heroes keep the streets safe from the notorious Komodo gang. Join the battle by bringing these warriors to life!

BODY MATTERS

When you can draw a figure with accurate proportions, your characters will look more realistic. Superheroes and villains often have exaggerated muscular physiques — some may even have animal or alien features!

The human body is symmetrical, with the bones and muscles on the left matching those on the right.

Men's bodies are often wide at the shoulders and chests, then narrower at the hips. Women's bodies are often narrow at the waist and wider at the hips, like the number 8.

All human bodies are about eight heads tall. The waist is about three heads down from the top of the body, and the hands reach midway down the thigh.

When you draw a person standing up straight, you should be able to draw a straight line from the top of their head down through their waist, to their knees, and through the center of their feet. Their shoulders should push out as far as their bottom, while their chest pushes out as far as their toes.

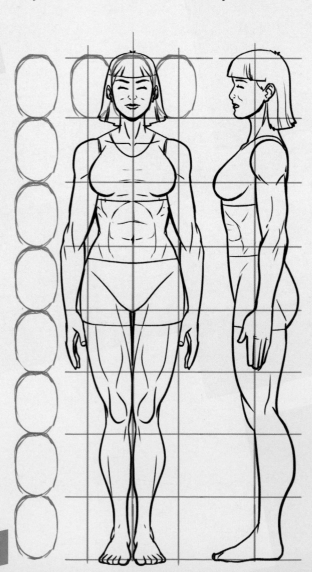

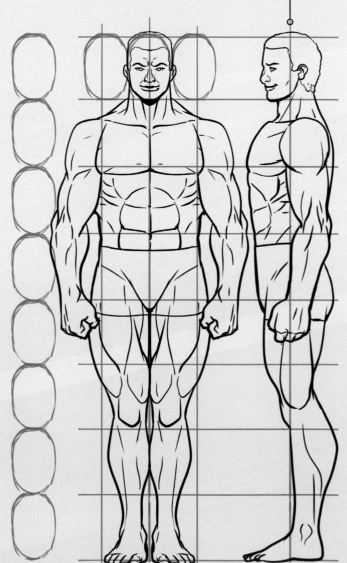

FACE TIME

Faces have their own proportions, with eyes and ears about halfway down the head. Here are average faces you can use for reference.

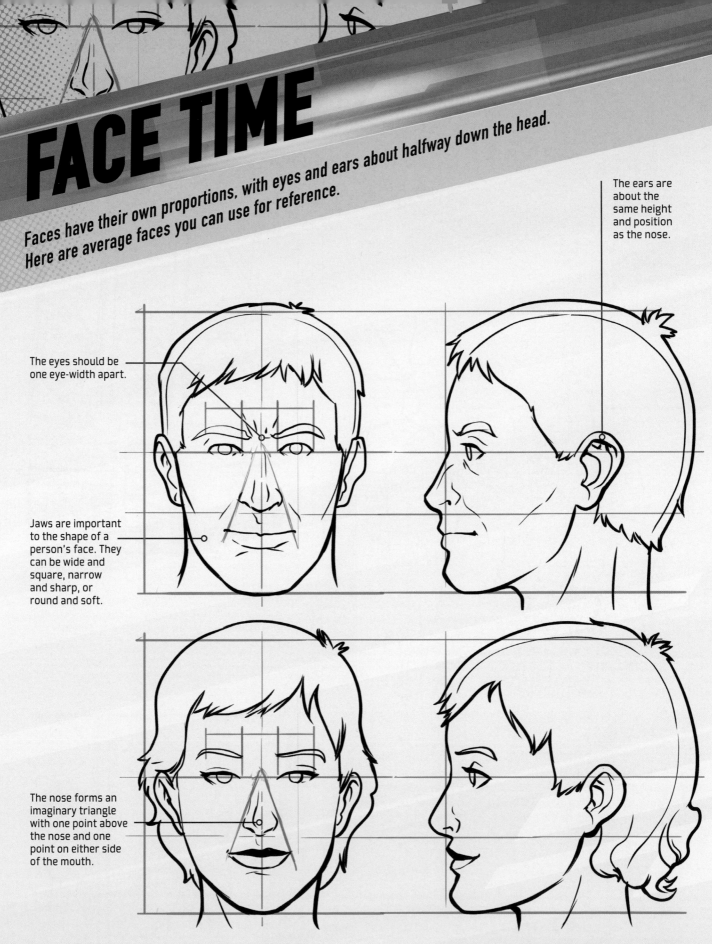

The eyes should be one eye-width apart.

Jaws are important to the shape of a person's face. They can be wide and square, narrow and sharp, or round and soft.

The nose forms an imaginary triangle with one point above the nose and one point on either side of the mouth.

The ears are about the same height and position as the nose.

Look at your friends' and family members' faces. You will see many variations. Sketch the details you see and study their hairstyles. You can use traits like these to make each of your comic characters unique.

FROM START TO FINISH

If you're brimming with ideas, you can jump straight into drawing your comic book. For most creators, a good page of comic art requires a bit of preparation.

PANEL 1 - THE VILLAIN AUTOMATOR - MALE, IN HI-TECH UNIFORM COVERED IN SENSORS AND DIGITAL READOUTS - DRIVES A ROBOTIC TANK THROUGH MANHATTAN, CAUSING DESTRUCTION. THE TANK HAS A BULLDOZER-LIKE VICE AT THE FRONT, POWERED BY HYDRAULICS, AND TWO ROBOTIC ARMS. ONE ROBOT ARM THROWS A CHUNK OF DEBRIS AT THE HERO MAMMOTH, KNOCKING HIM DOWN. SPACE FOR DIALOGUE FROM AUTOMATOR-WHO IS IN THE TANK'S DRIVING SEAT.

PANEL 1 DIALOGUE:
AUTOMATOR: CATCH!
MAMMOTH: OOF!

1. THE SCRIPT

First, plan your story. Think about the characters who appear in the adventure. What do they look like, what do they wear, and how do they behave? Then, write your story with notes on the action that will take place on each page.

2. THUMBNAILS

Now you can map out a page. These first small, rough sketches for page layouts are called **THUMBNAILS**. When you're happy with the layout, you can move to a larger sheet of paper and prepare for the finished artwork.

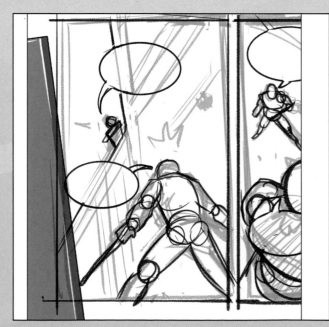

3. THE PANELS

Draw the panels lightly on the page and mark where the **SPEECH BALLOONS** will go. Then you can start drawing details in pencil, starting wherever you like on the page.

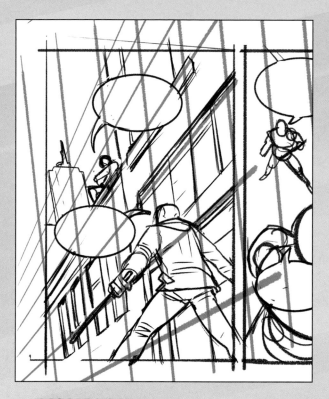

4. PERSPECTIVE

Guidelines for **PERSPECTIVE** help create a 3D environment for many scenes. You can start drawing your characters as stick figures so that you get their poses and positions right.

5. DIALOGUE

Draw the final details in pencil. Add ruled lines to the speech balloons and write the dialogue between them.

6. COLORING IN

Go over the pencil sketches in ink with a pen or brush, including the panels and speech balloons. Once the ink is dry, you can erase the pencil lines. Finally, it's time for the colors!

MODEL SHEETS

When you've come up with some exciting new characters, you'll want to make sure you always draw them right. Create a model sheet, like this, to show your characters from the front, side, and rear, for reference.

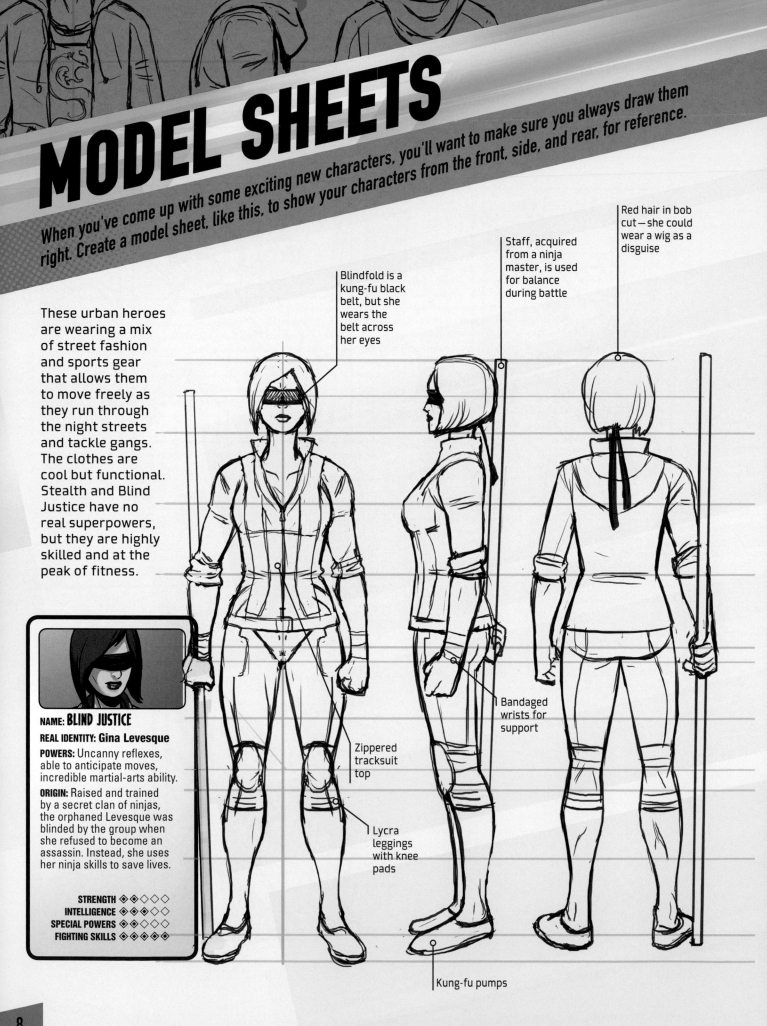

These urban heroes are wearing a mix of street fashion and sports gear that allows them to move freely as they run through the night streets and tackle gangs. The clothes are cool but functional. Stealth and Blind Justice have no real superpowers, but they are highly skilled and at the peak of fitness.

Blindfold is a kung-fu black belt, but she wears the belt across her eyes

Staff, acquired from a ninja master, is used for balance during battle

Red hair in bob cut—she could wear a wig as a disguise

Zippered tracksuit top

Lycra leggings with knee pads

Bandaged wrists for support

Kung-fu pumps

NAME: BLIND JUSTICE

REAL IDENTITY: Gina Levesque

POWERS: Uncanny reflexes, able to anticipate moves, incredible martial-arts ability.

ORIGIN: Raised and trained by a secret clan of ninjas, the orphaned Levesque was blinded by the group when she refused to become an assassin. Instead, she uses her ninja skills to save lives.

STRENGTH ◆◆◇◇◇
INTELLIGENCE ◆◆◆◆◇
SPECIAL POWERS ◆◆◇◇◇
FIGHTING SKILLS ◆◆◆◆◆

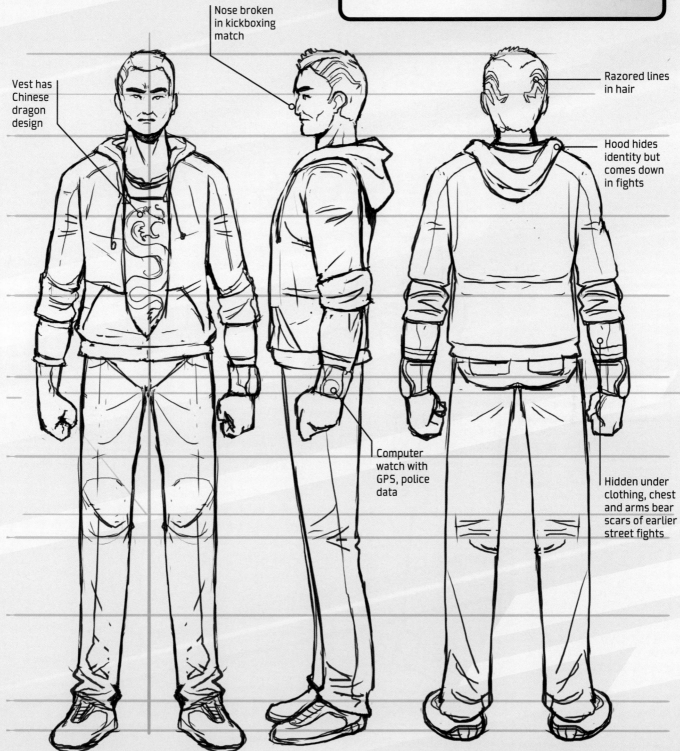

ORIGIN: After discovering that the police were controlled by criminals, forensic scientist and kickboxing champion Dasaolu chose to continue investigations as a nighttime vigilante.

NAME: STEALTH

REAL IDENTITY: Aaron Dasaolu

POWERS: Detective and martial-arts skills.

STRENGTH ◇◆◇◇◇
INTELLIGENCE ◇◆◇◆◇
SPECIAL POWERS ◆◇◇◇◇
FIGHTING SKILLS ◇◆◆◇◇

Nose broken in kickboxing match

Vest has Chinese dragon design

Razored lines in hair

Hood hides identity but comes down in fights

Computer watch with GPS, police data

Hidden under clothing, chest and arms bear scars of earlier street fights

MARTIAL ARTIST

When drawing a martial-arts hero, you need to think like a martial artist, considering the pose carefully. Put your hero in a calm, disciplined, and balanced position, alert and ready to defend or strike.

NAME: GOLDEN LOTUS

REAL IDENTITY: Unknown

POWERS: Martial-arts mistress of Qi — able to sense life energy and locate weak points on any opponent.

ORIGIN: Said to be an incarnation of the Southern Dragon goddess, Golden Lotus has studied how to channel the beast's legendary power.

STRENGTH ◈◈◇◇◇
INTELLIGENCE ◈◈◈◈◇
SPECIAL POWERS ◈◈◈◇◇
FIGHTING SKILLS ◈◈◈◈◈

1. WIRE FRAME
Using a pencil, lightly draw a stick figure showing your hero's action pose, with circles for each joint. Make sure the figure is correctly proportioned and balanced.

2. BLOCK FIGURE
Use basic shapes as the building blocks for the figure of Golden Lotus. Note how her shoulders tilt at the same angle as her raised arms, and her hands are at right angles to her arms.

TOP TIP

If you're not sure about a pose, try holding the position yourself. Does it feel natural? Is there a better way to pose your character?

3. ANATOMY

Lightly define Golden Lotus's slim and muscular body. Once you have the correct anatomy, you can sketch her costume, making her cloak's sleeves hang off her arms.

4. FINISHED PENCIL SKETCHES

Complete the pencil sketches, adding folds in Golden Lotus's cloak that curve away from her joints and where the material is tucked in. Draw her trident weapon attached by a strap and her lotus-symbol belt.

BALANCING ACT

NO

YES

YES   NO

Human figures have a center of gravity behind the belly button. For correct balance, this should be directly above where the body is supported on the ground. When standing on one leg, it is on the foot touching the ground. When standing on two, it is usually halfway between the feet.

5. INKS
Carefully go over your pencil sketches with dark ink lines, using a brush or pen. Fill in areas of black. Then, erase any pencil lines.

6. COLORS

Color in your figure, adding dark and light tones around the folds in the cloak to make it appear more 3D. Golden Lotus wears colors that suggest action. She can spring into combat mode in a second.

TOP TIP

Golden Lotus's clothes resemble those worn by martial-arts students. Dress your heroes in appropriate clothing for their fighting technique, without fussy extras that get in their way.

MASTERING THE MOVES

When planning a hand-to-hand fight, imagine you are directing actors in a movie, with each responding to one another's moves. Follow the action as Blind Justice and Hooded Crane begin battle.

1. In this step, both fighters are assessing each other. They stand in defensive positions, deciding who will make the first move. Arms are raised, anticipating a strike from the opponent's hands.

NAME: HOODED CRANE

REAL IDENTITY: Jian Lau

POWERS: Martial-arts master with a grip that is impossible to break.

ORIGIN: Rejected as leader of a ninja clan in favor of Blind Justice, Crane has since sought to prove himself better by defeating his rival.

STRENGTH ◇◇◇◇◇
INTELLIGENCE ◇◇◇◇◇
SPECIAL POWERS ◇◇◇◇◇
FIGHTING SKILLS ◇◇◇◇◇

2. The fight is like a dance, with both characters taking a turn to lead the action. Hooded Crane strikes first, kicking with his right foot to try to knock Blind Justice off balance. But Justice expected this move and swings aside, moving her weight to her right.

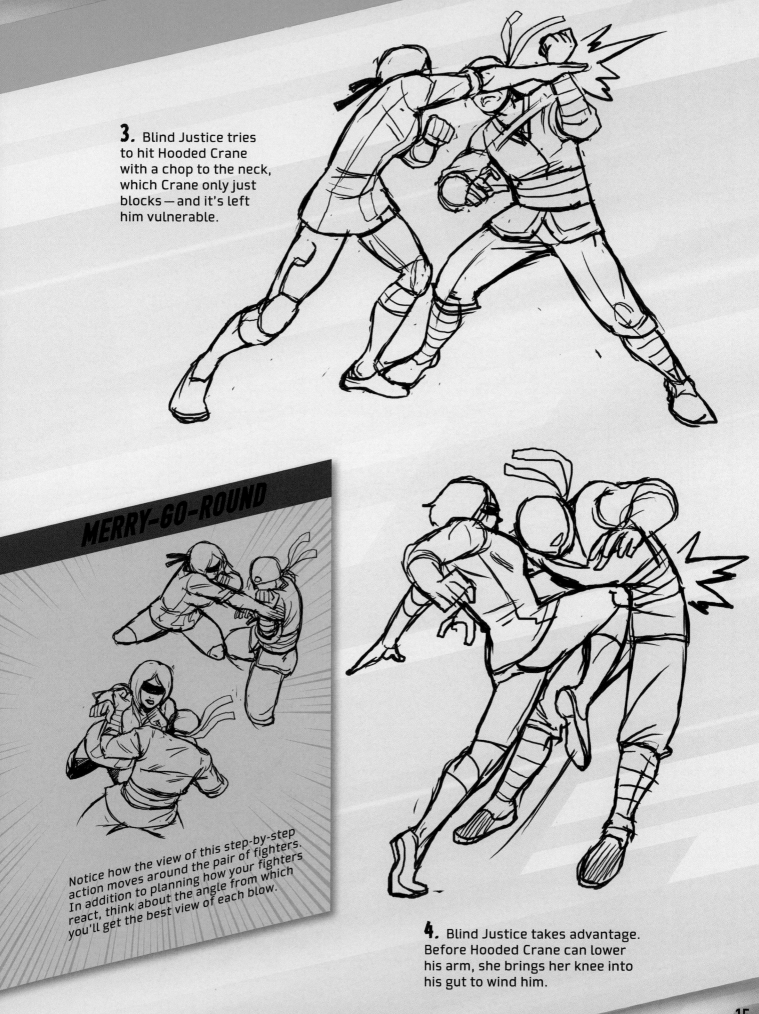

3. Blind Justice tries to hit Hooded Crane with a chop to the neck, which Crane only just blocks — and it's left him vulnerable.

MERRY-GO-ROUND

Notice how the view of this step-by-step action moves around the pair of fighters. In addition to planning how your fighters react, think about the angle from which you'll get the best view of each blow.

4. Blind Justice takes advantage. Before Hooded Crane can lower his arm, she brings her knee into his gut to wind him.

URBAN JUNGLE

A street-level hero needs a street. Here's how to use perspective lines to draw a realistic setting for your urban heroes and villains.

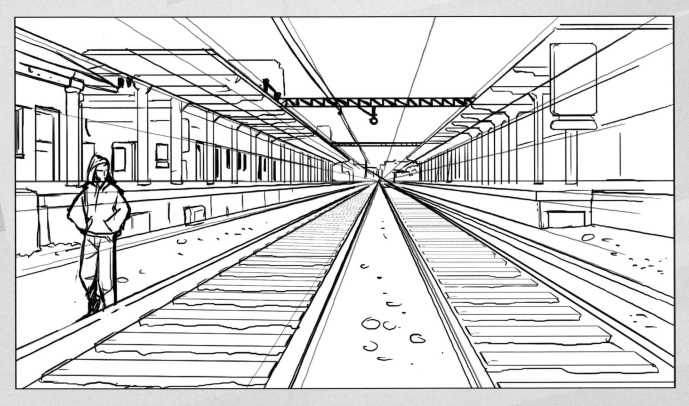

⌃ As objects get farther away, they appear smaller, like the rails on this track. The point at which the railroad track disappears is called the **VANISHING POINT**. The horizontal line in the distance, at the viewer's eye level, is called the **HORIZON LINE**.

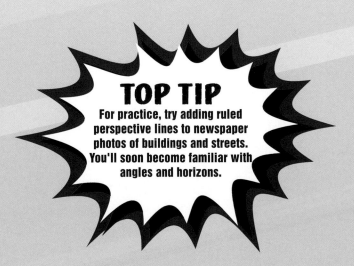

TOP TIP
For practice, try adding ruled perspective lines to newspaper photos of buildings and streets. You'll soon become familiar with angles and horizons.

▲ In this street scene, perspective lines drawn from the vanishing point on the horizon are used as guides to draw buildings and windows at the correct angle. This is a **ONE-POINT PERSPECTIVE**.

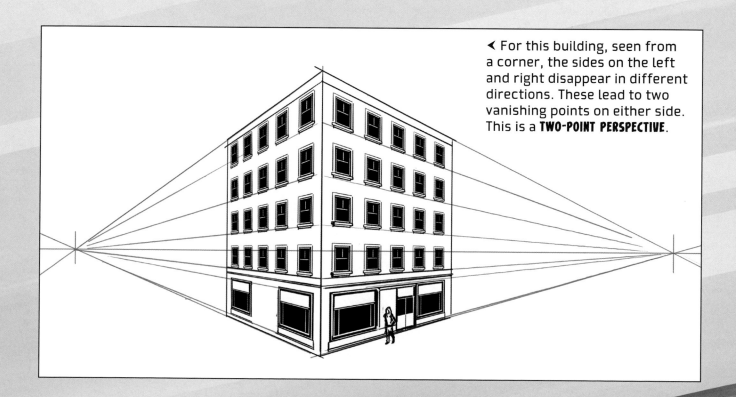

◄ For this building, seen from a corner, the sides on the left and right disappear in different directions. These lead to two vanishing points on either side. This is a **TWO-POINT PERSPECTIVE**.

PERSPECTIVES

This is an example of a **THREE-POINT PERSPECTIVE** with three vanishing points.

It's not just backgrounds that need a perspective. Using the same technique on a figure can produce a dramatic effect.

A dramatic three-point perspective is used here, where buildings are turned at different angles. The vertical perspective lines all point to the same vanishing point in the sky, but the horizontal lines cross one another to form a grid.

TOP TIP
When working on a scene with lots of depth, use a ruler to lightly draw the perspective lines before drawing the background.

HERO HQ

Home, sweet home! Now that you've seen how to create an exciting exterior, it's time to turn your attention to your heroes' headquarters. Enter the Loft, base for the Knight Patrol.

NAME: NOCTURNA

REAL IDENTITY: Alice Long

POWERS: Able to disappear into shadows and teleport between areas of darkness.

ORIGIN: Inherited the mystical Twilight Gem from her father, the Shadow Boxer.

STRENGTH ◆◇◇◇◇
INTELLIGENCE ◆◆◇◇◇
SPECIAL POWERS ◆◆◆◇◇
FIGHTING SKILLS ◆◇◇◇◇

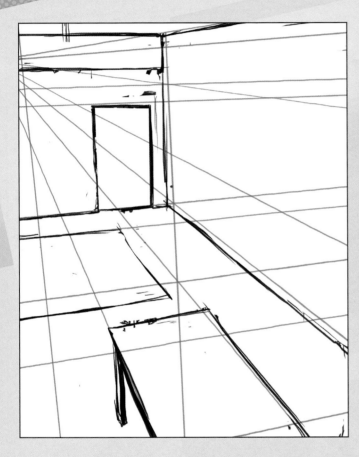

1. As with the street, perspective lines are used to work out angles for the floor and walls. A table in the room also follows the same perspective.

2. Chairs and other furniture can be placed in the scene. Compare the size of the chairs with the door on the far wall. Perspective makes the chairs look bigger in relation to the background features. Some extra decor, such as the weapon racks and lamps, is added to the apartment to suit its owner — the hero, Caracal.

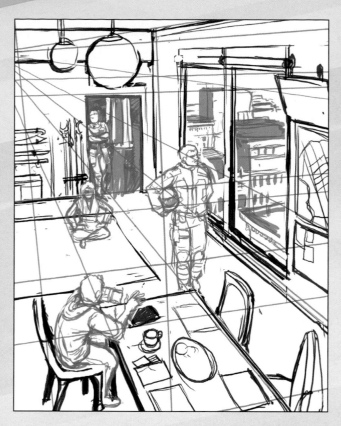

3. Now that the room is planned, the heroes can be positioned. Use perspective lines to help you draw the heroes at their correct relative sizes. Nocturna, the woman dressed all in black, is the tallest member of the Knight Patrol. Stealth and Blind Justice are seated. Blind Justice doesn't like chairs!

NAME: CARACAL

REAL IDENTITY: Josiah Ward

POWERS: Retractable claws in gloves and boots, for climbing and combat.

ORIGIN: After years on the wrong side of the law, former mercenary Ward chose to return to the streets of his birth and lead a war against crime.

STRENGTH ◇◇◇◇◇
INTELLIGENCE ◇◇◇◇◇
SPECIAL POWERS ◇◇◇◇◇
FIGHTING SKILLS ◇◇◇◇◇

4. Each member of the Knight Patrol interacts with the setting and the other characters. Consider what your characters are doing in each scene. Here, Caracal is looking out of the window while Stealth is drinking coffee and checking his computer watch.

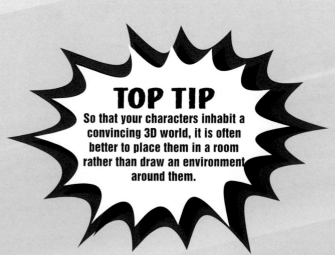

TOP TIP
So that your characters inhabit a convincing 3D world, it is often better to place them in a room rather than draw an environment around them.

SPEAK OUT!

So far, your urban heroes have been the strong and silent types. With some well-chosen words, you can make the action and dialogue leap off the page.

▲ Comic books use speech balloons to hold dialogue. Though you can vary the shapes, balloons tend to be oval, with a tail from the balloon pointing toward, but not touching, the mouth of the speaker. Words are usually in capital letters.

▲ Spoken words, such as the action on the page, should be read from top left to bottom right, so think ahead when you place your characters in a panel. Don't have their speech balloons crossing! Above is an example of what NOT to do.

▲ Be sure to allow enough room for the talking. Try not to cover up the characters with speech balloons! This example covers too much of the character's face.

NAME: THE DRAGON KING

REAL IDENTITY: Unknown

POWERS: Gangland boss who can hypnotize people with his ferocious mask.

ORIGIN: After a series of mysterious deaths of mob bosses, the Dragon King stepped forward to fill the void and rule Capital City's underworld.

STRENGTH ◆◆◆◇◇
INTELLIGENCE ◆◆◆◆◇
SPECIAL POWERS ◆◇◇◇◇
FIGHTING SKILLS ◆◆◆◇◇

THE DOCKS ARE NO SAFE PLACE TO WANDER AT NIGHT.

⌃ You can add a caption in a box to set a scene.

YOU SNEAK AROUND THE BACK.

I'M NOT SURE I CAN TRUST GOLDEN LOTUS.

NOCTURNA, GET DOWN!

HERE COMES SALAMANDER! LAY LOW! HE WON'T SUSPECT A THING!

YOU EXPECTING SOMEONE **ELSE?** THE SURPRISE IS ON **YOU!**

⌃ Speech balloons can be different shapes for different expressions:

·A dashed border for whispers.

·A cloud shape for thoughts.

·A starburst for shouts or screams.

⌃ When writing speech, use lightly ruled lines with some space between them. Write in the dialogue, then use an ellipse template or curve tool, if you have one, to draw the balloon borders.

⌃ Write in neat capitals and leave a border around the words inside the balloon. A technical pen is good for this. You can use a thicker pen to write bolder words for emphasis.

Finally, remember that comics are a visual medium. While words matter, don't forget to show your characters expressing themselves with their actions, too!

POINT OF VIEW

If you want to add extra dynamism to your comic book story, you need to choose some exciting viewpoints.

◄ The viewpoint is similar to a camera position in a movie. For the big dockside showdown between the Knight Patrol and the Lurker's mob, we need to choose a good viewpoint where we can see all the important action.

This first attempt is a low angle, from the dockside, as the boat crashes into the quay. This is what the gangsters see from their viewpoint, but the Knight Patrol is too distant in this view.

➤ This **BIRD'S-EYE VIEW** is more interesting, but we still feel too far from the action.

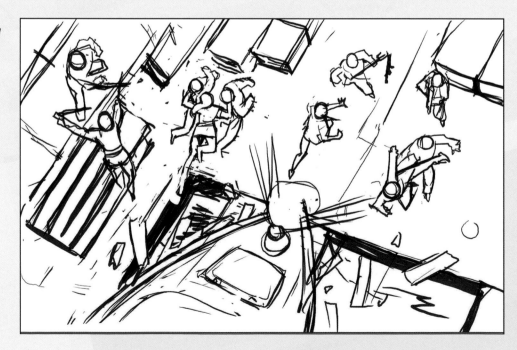

▲ This is better! We're right in the middle of the action here, as the Knight Patrol makes easy work of the Lurker and his mobsters. You can almost feel Caracal's kick making contact, and the viewpoint allows you to be led around the scene.

TOP TIP
A dramatic point of view looks great in one panel, but if you choose too many different views on one page, it can make the reader feel dizzy!

DOCKSIDE COMBAT

And here's the showdown at the docks in glorious inks and color.

STEP ASIDE, LOSER!

STEAL THE SPOTLIGHT!

Conversations in comics aren't just about speaking and listening. With the right choice of panels, you can plan your dialogue scenes for maximum visual impact.

When planning your comic book story, you need to choose which moments you want to show — to keep the story going — and how much you need to reveal in a panel.

The left-hand panel sets the exterior scene, but the right-hand panel is better, with both characters seen inside their HQ.

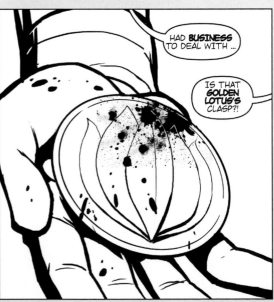

Stealth has brought something of importance to show Caracal, but you can't see it clearly in the left-hand panel. The close-up in the right-hand panel draws attention to the object — a blood-splashed clasp! Shocking!

IDEAS BOARD

Never be stuck for inspiration for your comic books. Look around you, and keep notes and sketches in your own ideas book. Here are some images and phrases that could inspire characters and stories.

> Jaws on each palm. Do not shake hands!

▲ Shellshock's armor is upgraded, but it takes control of his mind. How can he be stopped?!

> An ancient sword, possibly alien in origin, is unearthed by archaeologists.

▲ The Revealer comes from the future to announce the hero's death day.

TO BE CONTINUED...

Now it's over to you! We hope we've given you some ideas for stories and characters, and some good advice on how to create a professional-looking comic book story. But don't stop here — artists never stop learning!

➤ Carry a small sketchbook with you at all times. You never know when an idea will hit. Draw every day, even if it's just a doodle.

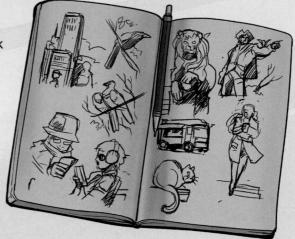

◄ Read plenty, and not just comics. Books are full of ideas, too, with rich characters and situations.

◄ Show your work to friends, share your drawings online, and go to comic conventions to show your art to professionals. Comic pros can give you tips on how to improve your work.

▼ Movies are a great source of inspiration. Pay attention to the direction and movement of the camera, and the way light and shadows create mood.

GLOSSARY

BIRD'S-EYE VIEW View looking down from above.

HORIZON LINE Where the horizon would appear in a view, usually at eye height.

MODEL SHEET A drawing of a character used as reference.

ONE-POINT PERSPECTIVE A perspective with parallel horizontal and vertical lines, plus one vanishing point.

PERSPECTIVE A way of representing three-dimensional (3D) objects in a picture.

SPEECH BALLOON A shape used in comic panels to hold character dialogue.

THREE-POINT PERSPECTIVE A perspective with three vanishing points.

THUMBNAIL A rough small-scale sketch used for planning a page layout.

TWO-POINT PERSPECTIVE A perspective with two vanishing points.

VANISHING POINT The point where perspective lines meet.

FURTHER INFORMATION

Book to read

Create Your Own Superhero Stories by Paul Moran (Buster Books, 2010)

DC Comics Coloring Book by DC Comics Warner Bros. (Studio Press, 2016)

Drawing Manga: Step by Step by Ben Krefta (Arcturus Publishing, 2013)

Stan Lee's How to Draw Superheroes by Stan Lee (Watson-Guptill, 2013)

The Super Book for Super-Heroes by Jason Ford (Laurence King, 2013)

Write and Draw Your Own Comics by Louise Stowell and Jess Bradley (Usborne, 2014)

Websites

PowerKids Press has developed an online list of websites related to the subject of this book. This site is updated regularly. Please use this link to access the list: **www.powerkidslinks.com/uca/urban**

INDEX

Published in 2018 by **The Rosen Publishing Group, Inc.**
29 East 21st Street, New York, NY 10010

CATALOGING-IN-PUBLICATION DATA

Names: Potter, William.
Title: Drawing urban heroes / William Potter and Juan Calle.
Description: New York : PowerKids Press, 2018. | Series: Ultimate comic art | Includes index.
Identifiers: ISBN 9781508154754 (pbk.) | ISBN 9781508154693 (library bound) | ISBN 9781508154570 (6 pack)
Subjects: LCSH: Heroes in art--Juvenile literature. | Figure drawing--Technique--Juvenile literature. | Comic books, strips, etc.--Technique--Juvenile literature.
Classification: LCC NC825.H45 P68 2018 | DDC 741.5'1--dc23

Copyright © 2018 Arcturus Holdings Limited

Text: William Potter
Illustrations: Juan Calle and Info Liberum
Design: Neal Cobourne
Design series edition: Emma Randall
Editor: Joe Harris

Manufactured in the United States of America

CPSIA Compliance Information: Batch BS17PK: For Further Information contact Rosen Publishing, New York, New York at 1-800-237-9932.